ZEBRAS PAINT THEMSELVES RAINBOW
Volume One

Silly Willy's WORLD

KATHRYN VELIKANJE
Illustrated by Nune Hovhannisyan

# LEVITY PRESS

© 2013 Levity Press

Illustrations by Nune Hovhannisyan

All rights reserved.

No part of this book may be reproduced in any matter whatsoever without the written consent of Levity Press, except in the case of brief quotations embodied in reviews.

This book uses OpenDyslexic. This font was created to help dyslexic readers. The heavy bottoms and unique character shapes help prevent letters and numbers from being confused.
Available at http://dyslexicfonts.com

Published by Levity Press
http://www.levitypress.com
Email: info@levitypress.com

ISBN 10: 1939896029
ISBN 13: 978-1-939896-02-5

Written for the children of China

DEDICATED

To Don -
    Who introduced me to these unusual,
    but oh so funny, names of animal groups.

To Michael Murphy -
    Who was the rock upon which I flourished,
    who taught so much by his silence,
    who was the bridge to my dreams.

To Melissa and Annie -
    Who never stop believing in me.

To GUS -
    Who is always there guiding me.

To Everyone -
    Who loves to laugh and shares my sense of humor.

Table of Contents

A Harem of Seals 1
An Ambush of Tigers 3
A Cute of Koalas 5
A Dazzle of Zebras 7
A Bellowing of Bullfinches 9
A Party of Pandas 11
A Rhumba of Rattlesnakes 13
An Intrusion of Cockroaches 15
A Crazy of Cats 17
An Implausibility of Gnus 19
A Murder of Crows 21
An Ugly of Walruses 23
A Fall of Lambs 25
An Ostentation of Peacocks 27
A Nursery of Raccoons 29
A Convocation of Eagles 31
A Congregation of Alligators 33
A Crash of Rhinos 35
A Superfluity of Nuns 37
A Rout of Wolves 39
A Stare of Owls 41
A Mob of Kangaroos 43
A Descent of Woodpeckers 45
A Wake of Buzzards 47
A Sleuth of Bears 49

A harem of seals,
too modest to play,
sun-bathed on soft cushions
in front of the bay.

Regal and shining,
they ate a fine meal:
octopus, lobster,
crabs, shrimp, squid and eel.

Atop a rock shelf,
apart from the rest,
they painted their toenails
and dressed in their best.

An ambush of tigers
was routed with glee,
chased back to the forest
by little old me.

I stabbed and I prodded,
I growled and I roared.
They crouched and deflated,
so much I got bored.

A cute of koalas
is a strange pair,
their little joeys
are born without hair.

Sleeping all day
and eating all night,
their brains are reduced
from a diet too light.

A bellowing of bullfinches roused me from bed and sent my hair flying high over my head.

A party of pandas pretended to play as jolly policemen that hot summer day.

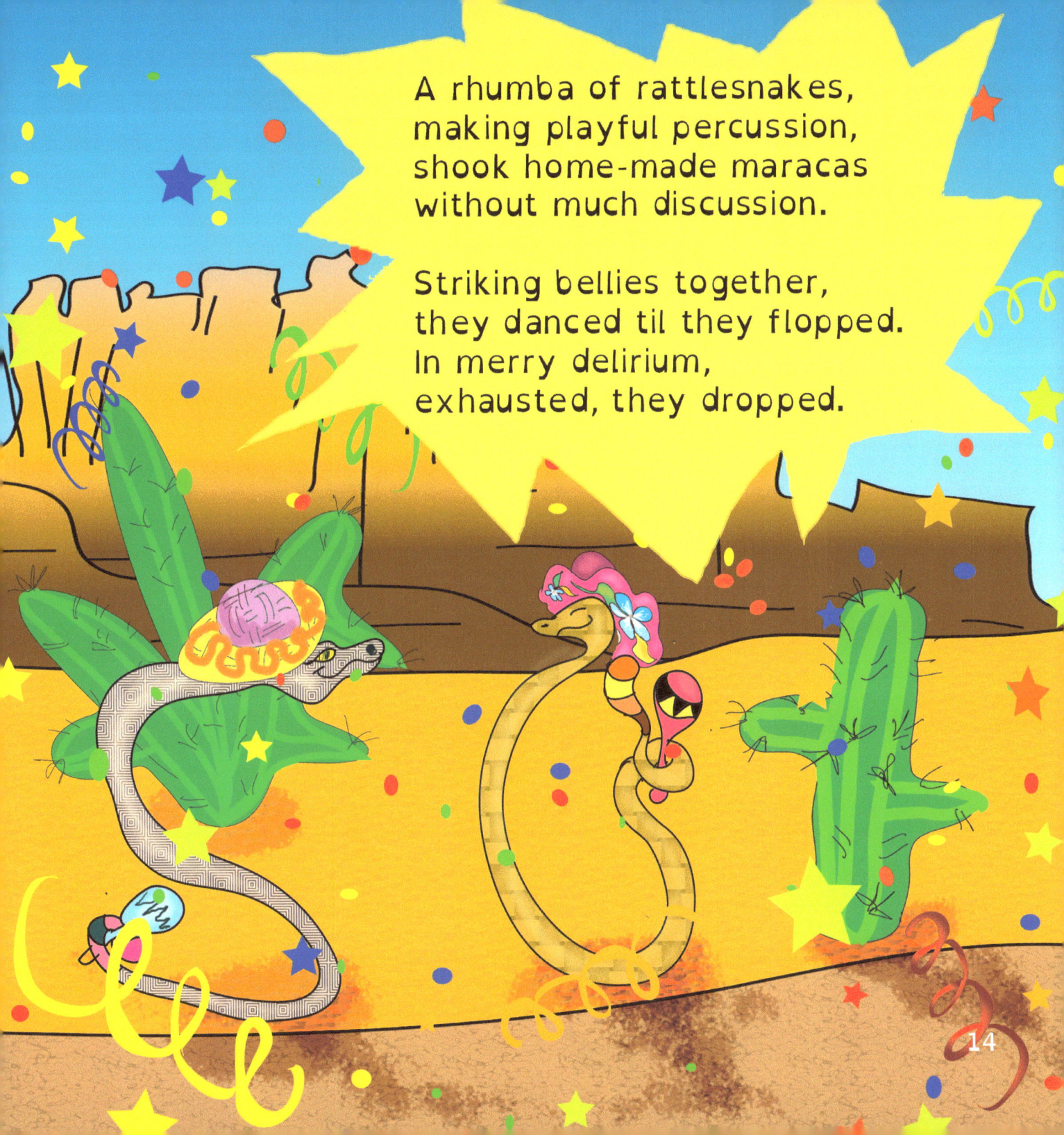

A rhumba of rattlesnakes,
making playful percussion,
shook home-made maracas
without much discussion.

Striking bellies together,
they danced til they flopped.
In merry delirium,
exhausted, they dropped.

An intrusion of cockroaches
swarmed under the bed
in a sea of destruction
that covered my head.

Black was all I could see,
black was all I could think,
as I tumbled and fumbled
and only could sink.

I thought I was dead
til I heard a strange sound,
a vacuum was sucking
them up from the ground.

An implausibility of gnus
blue, black, bearded and horned,
a million years old,
have never been scorned.

The ladies did love them,
dancing there under the sun,
each a fine soldier
who knew how to have fun.

An ostentation of peacocks
was a Medieval feast
fit for a king,
who usually ate beast.

The serfs ate chicken,
the gentry ate swan,
and kings ate peacocks
until early dawn.

Their plumage adorned
both ladies and tables,
and was a grand sight
worthy of fables.

A nursery of raccoons
slept in cribs and striped socks,
and stole in their masks
and opened up locks.

A congregation of alligators
sang a glorious song
of prayer and forgiveness
for all that was wrong.

Dressed in holiday clothes
and made up in their best,
they ate cake and cookies,
and acted like guests.

A rout of black wolves howled at the moon and kept me awake that night in June.

"You shush!" I yelled. "You go back to sleep now!" But on they continued and awakened the cow.

A mob of kangaroos
held a kick-boxing meet
and boxed with gloved hands
and sold every seat.

The joeys ate popcorn,
and other junk too,
while jumping in circles,
rooting their roos.

A descent of woodpeckers leveled the house in one day and left only a mouse on the pile to play.

A sleuth of bears
searched for their kin
who barely moved
their eyes, hands or chin.

They scoffed to see such lazy bears
and tried to rouse them from their lairs.
They did not want their friends to be
a sloth of bears, like you and me.

If you liked Silly's Willy's World,
other books by Kathryn Velikanje

 is for ALLIGATOR

 is for BOYS and BEES

 is for CRAZY CATS

 is for DRAGON

 is for ELEPHANT

 is for FACE

 is for GIRLY GIRLS

 is for HORSE

www.LevityPress.com
Kathryn.LevityPress@gmail.com

ABOUT THE AUTHOR

Kathryn is an American who has been teaching English in China since 2009. She graduated from the University of California at Santa Barbara with a Bachelor of Arts in Literature and has taught over 4500 ESL classes, from preschool through university as well as to teachers and doctors.

ABOUT THE ILLUSTRATOR

Nune Hovhannisyan was born in Yerevan, Armenia. She studied mathematics and chemistry, but realized that it wasn't the right choice. She has been drawing all her life and now has over 10 years experience as a children's illustrator, and the last 5 years has been working as a freelance illustrator. She has worked on and published over 40 illustrated children's books. She works mostly with digital illustration and drawing software like Photoshop and Illustrator, but also loves to work with traditional techniques, oil and acrylic painting, watercolors, and all drawing techniques. She loves creating illustrations that combine both traditional and digital mediums into colorful, playful and vibrant colors.
Her email is nuneo@mail.ru

www.ingramcontent.com/pod-product-compliance
Lightning Source LLC
Chambersburg PA
CBHW041533040426
42446CB00002B/75